A GUIDE FOR
MASTERS-ELECT
N P Halliday

(ii)

A GUIDE FOR
MASTERS-ELECT
N P Halliday

LEWIS MASONIC

(iv)

©1988
Dr N. P. Halliday
Published by **LEWIS MASONIC,** Ian Allan Regalia Ltd,
Terminal House, Shepperton, TW17 8AS
who are members of the Ian Allan Group.
First published in England in 1988

British Library Cataloguing in Publication Data
Halliday, N. P. (Norman P.)
A guide for masters elect.
1. Great Britain. Freemasons: Worshipful Masters. Duties — Manuals
I. Title
366'.1
ISBN 0-85318-159-4

Design and production by R. S. Design & Print
in association with Kent Art Printers

Illustrations from the Book of Constitution (B.O.C.)
United Grand Lodge of England.

CONTENTS Page

MASTER OF LODGE

Chapter One

THE MASTER'S ROLE

BROTHER READER, I would be delighted if your position in Lodge was that of newly appointed steward. However, the chances are that you are a Warden, hopefully the Junior Warden, wishing to pick up a few tips as your year as Master rapidly approaches.

The year that a brother spends as the Master of a Lodge should be the happiest and most enjoyable of his masonic career. In order that he gets the maximum pleasure and satisfaction from occupying the Chair of King Solomon, some preparation is necessary. It goes without saying that: the greater the preparation the greater the satisfaction — satisfaction not only to yourself but to the brethren of the Lodge.

Masonry is not about one's accomplishments nor indeed about self-satisfaction. Rather is it concerned with sharing those oft-quoted virtues: brotherly love, relief, and truth, and in a very real sense and not simply as a cliché. If ever there is a time in one's masonic career when one should practise such virtues, it is during one's Mastership.

Clearly a Master does not make nor break a Lodge but an effective Master can contribute greatly to the well-being of his Lodge. A succession of effective Masters can indeed establish a Lodge as one which is attractive by membership or, at the very least, one to be visited. Such a Lodge is obviously one where the ceremonial ritual is of a very high standard, but, perhaps of greater importance, it is a Lodge where a brother can experience in a very tangible way those features of Freemasonry that make it the warm, caring society of men which continues to thrive despite all attempts through the ages to discredit the organisation.

Achieving these aims during one's Mastership will not be easy, and it must be said that not every Master actually achieves these objectives. In many cases the lack of achievement is the result of lack of preparation. That preparation must include learning the ritual for the ceremonies in the Temple, but it must go much wider than the ceremonial ritual if one wishes to approach the Chair with confidence.

Every moment spent in preparation is worthwhile. Brethren past and present will have worked hard to have made the Lodge a success and their accumulated efforts will contribute to the success of the year as Master.

The mantle of Master carries with it a legacy which should not be ignored. Many Masters find that, contrary to what they expected, the ceremonies are almost the easiest part of their Mastership. The responsibility of ruling and directing a Lodge cannot be successfully discharged from an expert understanding of the ceremonies alone. Fortunately, the Master, although carrying ultimate responsibility, is assisted by the Officers and past-Masters of the Lodge, many of whom will be experienced masons of long-standing. Such a team exists in every Lodge and what is required is for the Master to assume his proper role of **leader of the team.**

This booklet concerns itself with matters relating to Craft masonry. Chapter 12 gives some details about Royal Arch Masonry. There can be little doubt that one's understanding and enjoyment of Craft masonry is increased by having been exalted into Royal Arch. It must be open to doubt as to whether a Master is fully equipped to discharge his commitment in the third degree to ". . . assist the brethren to repair that loss", unless he has been so exalted.

MASTER OF LODGE

Chapter Two

MAKING A START

E VERY BROTHER who wishes to progress through the various offices is urged to turn his attention to the Book of Ritual as soon as he is appointed Steward, if not before. The most effective way of mastering the ritual is by attendance at class (or Lodge) of instruction. Attending a class of instruction is not only a painless way of learning the ritual that is part of each office, it is a means of getting to know his fellows. The camaraderie that develops at class of instruction stands him in good stead when the time comes to fulfil the role of Master. The value of such camaraderie cannot be over stated.

It is natural that any brother holding office concentrates on the "work" of his particular office, leaving the ceremonies "till later". Brethren are well advised to study at least two of the degree ceremonies early in their career. To be able to perform two of the degree ceremonies at class of instruction, preferably before one is a warden, will ensure that much of the stress is removed from being Master of a Lodge. The year as Master is always a very busy time, without adding the worry of having to start from scratch with the ceremonies.

Many lodges have a policy whereby brethren must show evidence of masonic ability by insisting that they perform two of the degree ceremonies at class of instruction before occupying the office of Junior or Senior Warden. The purpose of such a policy is to benefit the well-running of the Lodge and to assist the brother concerned to get the best from his year as Master. All brethren will have heard successive immediate past-masters stating that their year as Master was the shortest of their masonic career. Obviously, it was not, but such statements should warn younger brethren that the Master's year is a busy one.

The best advice to any brother aspiring to the Master's Chair is to study assiduously the book of ritual until he is ready to perform at least two of the degree ceremonies before occupying the office of Warden. It is suggested that to get maximum benefit, brethren should attempt the First and Third degrees. A brother need not be word-perfect, but having actually performed the ceremony in class of instruction will give him the added confidence of understanding the 'workings' in Temple, which cannot be learned from the book.

The message to a brother wishing to progress is, therefore, a simple one:-

(i) attend class of instruction as often as possible

(ii) get to know the brethren who will form your 'team' in years to come

(iii) learn and perform at least two ceremonies.

There is, therefore, no need to make further reference to the ceremonial ritual in this booklet.

The greater a brother's masonic knowledge, the better will be his understanding of what is involved in any of the ceremonies. The easiest way to increase his understanding is by visiting other lodges where the variations in the workings will reinforce the meaning or cause him to ask questions, thereby increasing his knowledge.

There is a considerable library of masonic literature which can be obtained from most suppliers of masonic regalia. The lodge secretary or preceptor of class of instruction will be able to advise on suitable publications. A brother should be aware that his reading does not lead to confusion regarding the lodge's method of working. Many lodges have their own variations in working, sometimes great, sometimes small, but it is those differences which make Freemasonry so interesting. Once a lodge has established its individual pattern of performing the ritual, this is the 'correct' working for that particular lodge. Obviously the differences found in a lodge's working cannot be so great that it cannot conform to the accepted ritual, be it Emulation or other working.

Any brother interested in widening his masonic knowledge is well-advised to join the Quatuor Coronati Correspondence Circle. Members of the Circle receive annually a volume of lodge transactions containing the main lectures of that year. Membership of the Circle also brings with it other privileges (for details see annex). There is also a magazine for Freemasons entitled *Masonic Square* which contains articles of general interest and information of value to masons, (for details see annex). The London Grand Rank Association publishes a quarterly bulletin designed to enlighten and entertain Freemasons (for details see annex). Another masonic correspondence circle is the Dormer Masonic Study Circle who also hold regular meetings at Great Queen Street. (For details see annex).

An essential part of any mason's reading matter must be a regular perusal of the Lodge Bye-laws and the Book of Constitutions. The booklet **Information for the Guidance of Members of the Craft** cannot be too highly recommended and is a valuable source of information on any difficulties that may arise.

STEWARD

SENIOR WARDEN

Chapter Three

MASTER-ELECT

IN A LODGE where it is the established custom for officers by means of normal progression to reach the Master's chair, a brother should plan accordingly. It is of course, the Master's prerogative to appoint officers of his choosing (except the Treasurer and Tyler) — Rule 104, but in the normal course of events this will be by steady progression.

The election of the Master for the ensuing year is by ballot in open lodge at the meeting preceding the installation meeting, (B o C Rule 105).

It follows that the Master-Elect has very little time in which to prepare for his installation and the appointment of his officers. Clearly, if a Master-Elect is to become an effective Master he must have started his preparation much in advance of his election. It may sound presumptious, but a brother who wishes to be a successful Master should begin planning for his year, and the officers he will appoint, whilst he is still senior deacon. At such an early stage in his career he may wish to keep such planning to himself but by the time he is junior warden his plans should be at such a stage of development that he can seek the advice, in confidence, of the senior past masters. During his year as senior warden, and for a variety of reasons, his plan must be finalised.

The Master-Elect must obviously turn his attention first to the regular offices which must be filled. The regular offices are: The Master, two Wardens, Treasurer, Secretary, two Deacons, Inner Guard, and Tyler. The Master, Treasurer and Tyler are, of course, elected by the Brethren. He will then consider how best to fill the additional offices. Under rule 104(a) of the B o C, the Master is permitted to appoint additional officers, these being: Chaplain, Director of Ceremonies, Charity Steward, Almoner, Organist, Assistant-Secretary and Stewards, but no others.

It is not essential to fill all the additional offices, if there are problems in finding a brother able and willing to take on a particular office. Included among the additional offices is that of the Director of Cermonies. Given the important role the D C plays in ensuring that the ceremonies in the temple are performed with decorum, are in keeping with the particular ritual and also run smoothly, it is difficult to visualise a craft lodge without a D C. The Master-Elect is well-advised to consider the office of D C in the same way as he would the regular offices.

The Master-Elect should remember that no brother may hold two regular offices in the Lodge at one and the same time. Should it be necessary and in the interest of the Lodge the Master may appoint a brother to both a regular and an additional office. At this point it is perhaps worth mentioning that the I P M is not an officer of the Lodge. A brother becomes the I P M of the Lodge by virtue of his having vacated the Master's chair after completing his term in office and having installed his successor. It follows that in the absence of the I P M there cannot be an acting-I P M, although a past master may fill-in, performing the tasks normally performed by the I P M, (rule 104 (f)).

Most provinces publish a Masonic Year Book which gives details, including the officers and members of each Lodge in that Province. The time-scale of the preparation of the Year Book is such that a number of lodges will not have elected the Master for the ensuing year at the time of going to print. If the Year Book is to be of any value the senior warden will have to name his officers in anticipation of being elected. Fortunately, the Year Book will not normally be published until after the election of the Master, so that no embarrassment should arise from the senior warden having selected his officers in anticipation of his being elected.

The senior warden will wish to take soundings of all existing officers to ensure that circumstances have not changed, such that some may no longer wish to progress. Having informally confirmed that the brethren will accept the offices to be offered to them, it is the usual custom in many lodges for the senior warden to write to the respective brethren, formally making an offer of the office shortly after his election as Master-Elect.

It is at the sole discretion and power of the Master to appoint all the officers not subject to election (ie the Treasurer and Tyler). Rule 104(e). The Master-Elect will no doubt wish to take the advice of the senior past-masters and the Lodge Committee in such appointments. It is the usual custom for lodges to call a meeting of the Lodge Committee specifically to "meet the Master-Elect" and to offer any advice that he may require, relative to the appointment of the officers for the ensuing year. It is usual for the list of officers to be confirmed at that meeting. The Secretary and D C can then make the necessary arrangements for the installation meeting, and for reporting as necessary to Provincial Grand Lodge and Grand Lodge, the agreed changes in the officers of the Lodge.

Although from perusal of lodge summonses it may appear that the appointment of officers is a simple matter, that one regularly moves up a place, and that for no obvious reason a past master is appointed occasionally to perform a particular office which is not part of the ladder of progression. If only it were so simple. It must be a fortunate, and indeed a very rare lodge where problems surrounding the filling of the respective offices do not arise from time to time, if not regularly each year.

When considering the appointment of officers, the Master-Elect must not only consider what is best for his year, but must also have the long term well-being of the Lodge uppermost in his mind. It may be that a particular brother has an expert knowledge or a real ability to fit an important office, one that is not 'vacant' during the coming year but could be expected to be vacant in the future. In such cases it may be necessary, for the good of the Lodge, to plan the offices around that brother.

Decisions about the filling of offices must obviously be taken with the future of the Lodge in mind, but the morale, welfare, and satisfaction of the brethren must also be given very careful consideration. An attractive feature of Freemasonry is the ability of a member of a private lodge to progress to membership of Provincial and/or Grand Lodge, (see B o C). Such progression may extend further in the form of an appointment to an actual office, an active rank, or appointment to a past rank. Progression to active or past offices of either Lodge is usually by selection based on a brother's demonstrable good works but not exclusively to Freemasonry. Obviously, as a past master holding an office in one's own lodge and discharging the responsibility of that office in an effective fashion, is a means of improving one's chances of such selection, a worthy objective. The Master-Elect should therefore give much thought to the filling of additional offices with past masters, particularly those who have demonstrated their commitment to the Lodge. If at all possible the past masters who have not yet earned Provincial honours should be given preference over those who have been so honoured.

JUNIOR WARDEN

Chapter Four

INSTALLATION OF THE NEW MASTER

THE DAY FOR WHICH most master masons have waited is the day of installation as Master of their Lodge. To enjoy that event to the full, preparation is necessary. The Master-Elect must be able to assume his role as Master and to take control of the remainder of the meeting, and the festive board which follows. The Master-Elect will have prepared himself for the appointment and investiture of his officers, but he may not have given much thought to the normal business of the Lodge. The Master-Elect should brief himself on the business items with which he will have to deal. Custom dictates how many of these items should be considered and the Master should be familiar with such custom. If he is not, he may find himself at something of a loss and the business of the lodge may come to a grinding halt whilst the Master gets guidance from the I P M or nearby past masters. These 'little' hiccoughs can mar the start of the Master's year, and can so easily be avoided. If in any doubt, consult the Secretary. Indeed it is a wise Master who makes a point of discussing the agenda with the Secretary prior to the meeting.

The appointment and investiture of officers should be a very pleasing start to the Master's year, since it is the bringing together of his 'team' for the year and makes public the fruits of all the discussions and thoughts the Master-Elect has had prior to this moment. The procedure although formal, is one to be enjoyed by Master, Officers, and Brethren alike. It is more likely to be enjoyable if the Master is completely confident that he knows the ritual to be followed and the significance of the words used. Such confidence ensures smooth running, but more importantly, it allows the introduction of personal touches which add to the enjoyment.

The ritual book gives details of the actual closing of the degrees and of the Lodge, and need not be repeated here. It is perhaps worth mentioning the place of the National Anthem if, as is the custom in most lodges, the National Anthem is to be sung. The Master or D C should inform the brethren that the National Anthem is to be sung and that it will be followed by the closing hymn. The reason for having the anthem before the closing hymn, is that the reverse takes more time and means the "Procession" has to stand to attention during the anthem thus delaying the procession actually forming as is the normal custom during the closing hymn.

Finally, do not forget to take the Warrant of the Lodge with you as you leave the Temple, and remember to give it to the Secretary for safe-keeping. **The safe-keeping of the warrant is your responsibility whilst you hold the office of Master.**

MASTER OF LODGE

Chapter Five

THE FESTIVE BOARD

IN THIS BOOKLET stress is laid on the value of preparation in order to enjoy one's year as Master and, perhaps of greater importance, that the year for the Lodge is a success. There can be few master masons who would not accept that succcessful working in the temple requires considerable preparation both in the years leading up to, and during one's mastership. What is often not recognised is that success at the Festive Board requires a fair amount of thought and preparation and in the absence of such preparation the Festive Board can be a disaster, despite the excellence of the meal, wine and company. It is often said and not without some justification, that a Master can have great popularity and can be a success as Master because of the way he hosts the Festive Board. Equally, a Master who is an excellent ritualist may, by paying insufficient attention to the Festive Board, fail to achieve such success. The wise Master therefore views the Festive Board as an essential part of his year and worthy of his full attention and preparation. The recipe for success is therefore excellence in ritual, a relaxed and friendly manner and considerate hosting at the Festive Board.

In advance of the meeting there are certain aspects of the Festive Board which the Master should reflect upon, they are:

a) **Wine taking**
b) **Formal toasts**
c) **Response to the toast to the Worshipful Master**
d) **Toast to visitors and response**
e) **Other toasts**

a)   Wine taking

A great deal has been said and written about wine-taking over the years. The emphasis has been on reducing the number of wine-takings, the benefits of which are obvious.

Wine-taking is however a popular custom with many attractions if carried out in moderation. If wine-taking is to be a feature of your Festive Board then careful thought should be given to ensure that you include all those who deserve to be singled out; and of equal importance to ensure that you do not inadvertently leave a brother out of the wine-taking. Wine-taking is entirely at the discretion of the Master but, as with all things masonic, there are customs: when there are official visitors representing Grand Lodge or Provincial Grand Lodge it is customary to take wine with them before taking wine with your Wardens. It is not the usual custom to take wine with Grand Officers if they are members of one's own Lodge.

b)   Formal Toasts
Do not start until Grace has been recited or sung.

It is customary in most workings for the responsibility for proposing the main toasts at the Festive Board to fall to the Master. Whatever else was going on during wine-taking it is essential, during the formal toasts, that the Festive Board is tyled. This ensures that only masons are present and allows masonic fire after each toast. At this point in the evening's festivity, the Master must introduce an element of control to ensure decorum during these formal toasts.

The formal toasts (as the name applies) should be kept **strictly** formal so that gavelling when the brethren are still standing, ie gavelling immediately after one toast and before the next, is to be condemned and gives the impression that you want to get it over or that the toasts are not sincere. Let the brethren sit down and give a very short pause between toasts BUT make the pause short in order to keep control.

c)   Response to the Toast to the Worshipful Master
Since the Master will have to respond to this toast at each Festive Board it is no bad thing to give some thought to his response in advance. It may be possible to identify a theme which can be enlarged upon at each successive Festive Board. In the absence of a theme there may well be a message the Master would like to get across to the brethren and the success in doing so will be increased by some thought in advance. Even where a Master has no particular theme or message to get across, it still pays dividends to give some thought to what one may say in responding. There is nothing worse than the festivities being interrupted in order that The Worshipful Master can deliver a boring response to which no thought has been given. However little one proposes to say, do give some advanced thought to what you do say, if for no other reason than to avoid inadvertently upsetting a brother.

d) Visitors' Toast

It is the normal custom for this toast to be proposed by a brother other than the Master. The longer the proposer is given to prepare for this toast the more likely it is that the toast will have the desired effect, both in terms of entertainment and sincerity. There is no reason why a proposer cannot be given weeks in which to prepare. Equally, if one has regular visitors, one can give a visitor long notice in which to prepare a reply. Good toasts and replies add greatly to the enjoyment of a Festive Board, and all that can be done to this end, should be done.

e) Other Toasts

Amongst the other toasts that may be given at the Festive Board is that to the Initiate. Such a toast is a clear example where good notice to the proposer must be given, in order that such an important toast is delivered to the best advantage. Apart from giving the proposer good notice, the selection of the proposer is crucial. For such an important toast this must be an experienced mason.

On Installation evenings there is an important toast for the newly installed Master's attention, and that is the toast to the Immediate Past and Installing Master.

During the year the Master will wish to include the toast to The Masonic Charities, this affords the Charity Steward the opportunity to encourage greater participation in the charities.

Procedure at the Festive Board

On being received at the Festive Board, the new Master should gavel without undue delay and should then say Grace, or invite the Chaplain to do so. Grace normally takes the form: "For what we are about to receive may the G A O T U make us truly thankful and ever mindful of the needs of others".

When you sit down and get into conversation with the Provincial Grand Master or his representative, you can be forgiven if it slips your mind that you have work to do. During the Festive Board you will need to maintain some degree of control so that the wine-taking and formal toasts go smoothly.

You should begin the wine-taking as soon as the first course has been consumed. You may get two or even three wine-takings before soup if you are lucky. It is important to avoid taking wine during the main course for nothing spoils the evening, or ruins the digestion, as effectively as such a practice. It is important however, to keep up the pace of wine-taking and the formal toasts. If one drags out the toasts, control of the Festive Board may be lost and the interest of the brethren allowed to wander.

A word about the gavel: **remember you, and you alone use the gavel.** The Master's single knock is responded to by the Senior Warden and Junior Warden in turn. When you get to the Tyler's toast, it is two knocks with the gavel, to which the Wardens do not respond.

The gavel is a means of getting the attention of the brethren and maintaining order. It is not necessary to gavel loudly, for repeated loud gavelling is most disturbing and is a frequent cause of complaint. When the Master or I P M rises the brethren will respect the "Top Table" and silence will prevail. If silence does not prevail it should not be necessary to call attention to the 'Gavel', a short pause before speaking usually does the trick. Respect for the Master is not increased in proportion to the noise he makes, so do not deafen the brethren.

Soon after the meal has started, and before the wine-taking begins, the Master should ensure that "The Columns are charged". The I P M normally performs this task by rising, after the Master has gavelled, and asking:

"Bro Wardens, how do you report your respective columns?" To which the Senior Warden replies, "Fully (or All) charged in the West, Brother I P M". The Junior Warden replies in a similar fashion, "Fully (or All) charged in the South, Brother I P M".

The wine-taking can then proceed. The announcements of wine-takings are usually made by the I P M (or D C). The wine-taking list will normally take the form:

1. The Wardens
2. Representatives of Grand, or Provincial Grand Lodges
3. Visiting Grand Officers
4. Masters of other Lodges
5. The I P M
6. Bro Initiate/Bro who was passed/Bro who was raised
7. The Visitors
8. All the Brethren (request that they remain seated)
9. The Tyler

Other wine-takings may be indicated such as the presence of the Provincial Grand Master or his representative. The Master may also wish to take wine with an officer or brother who has assisted in the ceremony. Other brethren such as a visiting organist who has assisted, some special circumstance and on particular evenings, the Officers of the Lodge.

On completion of the dinner, before coffee is served, the Master should gavel, rise and announce "Brethren, pray silence for Grace"; or "Brethren, we will now sing Grace".

After Grace, all should then sit. The next item is the Loyal Toast, and whatever may be the procedure for other toasts, when Loyal Toast is proposed, all should rise as a mark of respect.

When the Master has gavelled, the I P M or D C will rise, call for silence saying "Brethren, pray silence for the W M", or the Master may rise unannounced, and propose "The Loyal Toast". There is no need for elaboration in proposing the Loyal Toast, indeed such elaboration could be improper. The accepted form of proposal is: "Brethren, the Queen and the Craft".

The Brethren will rise and if the National Anthem is to be sung, glasses are left on the table. After the National Anthem the brethren raise their glasses and toast "The Queen and the Craft".

The Master then calls for "Fire".

If the National Anthem has been sung in the Temple, it is not normally sung again at the Festive Board.

The next toast is "The M W Grand Master". After this toast the Master gives the Brethren permission to smoke.

Smoking should not be permitted until after this toast.

When the Provincial Grand Master, or his representative is present, the Master may delay permission to smoke until after the toast to the Provincial Grand Master.

The toasts will then proceed in the usual way, preferably without lengthy pauses between toasts. The formal toasts are:

1. The Queen and the Craft
2. The Most Worshipful the Grand Master
3. The Most Worshipful Pro Grand Master
   The Right Worshipful Deputy Grand Master
   The Right Worshipful Assistant Grand Master, and
   the rest of the Grand Officers, Present and Past
4. The Provincial Grand Master
5. The Deputy Provincial Grand Master
   The Assistant Provincial Grand Master(s) and
   the rest of the Provincial and District Grand Officers, Present and Past
   of this or any other Province or District and holders of London Grand Rank.

6. The Worshipful Master
7. The Installing Master (on Installation Meetings)
8. The Initiate
9. The Visitors
10. Absent Brethren
11. The Tylers Toast

There are other toasts such as Masonic Charities, Officers of the Lodge etc.

The toast to Absent Brethren is usually given at 9pm, though this is not essential, it must not however be given until after the Loyal Toast and the Toast to the Grand Master. The Tylers toast brings the Festive Board to a close.

The title Pro Grand Master causes some Brethren difficulty. Where the Grand Master is a member of the Royal Family, a Pro Grand Master may be appointed to represent the Grand Master on appropriate occasions. Given the pressures on a Royal Grand Master, and for the effective management of Grand Lodge, much of the work of Grand Lodge is taken forward on the Grand Master's behalf and approaches to the Grand Master are through the Pro Grand Master.

It is the custom of many Lodges to invite the ladies to join their husbands, boy-friends and relatives after the Festive Board is over. This custom is to be applauded for it involves the ladies in the evening's activities bringing pleasure to all concerned. They must not however, be admitted until the Festive Board activities have been completed, nor indeed must any non-mason.

The custom in its various forms is long established and well-documented from the early days of Freemasonry. It must be stressed however, that such participation by non-masons must only be after the completion of all masonic aspects of the Festive Board.

Chapter Six

WORK IN THE TEMPLE

LEARNING the ritual is not easy. Performing the ceremony in Temple is even less so.

Every Master quickly learns how easy it is to be thrown by a minor unplanned 'event' in lodge. To reduce to a minimum such minor events, attention must be given to the work to be dispatched during that evening in Temple. Before joining the in-going procession, make sure you have the warrant, the summons, a copy of the Bye-Laws and any notes you may require during the meeting.

The meeting normally begins by the brethren singing the Opening Ode. **The warrant of the Lodge is then displayed.** The Master will then proceed to open the lodge in the First Degree. At this juncture many Masters make a point of formally welcoming the visitors. It should be noted that this is the earliest point in the proceedings that the Master can welcome visitors if he wishes the fact to be recorded in the Minutes.

The Master can be confident that the Secretary will have organised the business of the meeting. The Director of Ceremonies will have checked that all the officers are present, that all is in readiness for the ceremony, and that the candidate has arrived. A Master with such support may feel that he need only concentrate on the ceremony. There are however a few points which may arise and are frequent causes of doubt and confusion to a new Master. Where a Master is confident about the proper course of action the effect is impressive and the smooth running of the meeting maintained. A few of these points now follow, but it should be stressed that the Secretary or Director of Ceremonies, will normally have these under control.

The purpose of mentioning them here is not to suggest that the Master usurps the duties of these officers. Where a Master is in doubt on any points of procedure and consults with the I P M, D C or Secretary then all will be well. The potential for embarrassment arises when the Master is in doubt and gives a ruling in Temple without checking the procedure with these officers. It is to avoid such embarrassment — not to preclude consultation that they are now mentioned.

Perhaps it is best to begin with those points that can arise regarding regalia.

Regalia

In inclement weather the Master may decide to allow the brethren to dispense with wearing of gloves. *This gesture does not normally apply to the officers and never to the Master or the Wardens if performing a ceremony.* The Master and Wardens must never remove their gloves to entrust candidates.

Now to collars: All officers must wear the collar of the office they hold. Where an officer holds more than one office he should wear both collars, with the senior collar outermost. Past-masters holding office will in addition wear the appropriate past master's collar. On the question of whether a brother who is standing in for an absent officer, should wear the collar of that office, or not, is less straight forward. Rulings differ in the various Provinces about the wearing of collars in such circumstances. Where there is no difference of opinion between the Provinces is where a brother stands in and performs the duties of a particular office whilst the regular officer is present in lodge. In such circumstances the collar of that office must *not* be worn. In the case where the regular officer is absent there is no constitutional rule and practice varies between provinces and indeed between lodges in provinces. In some provinces a brother having been appointed and invested with the collar, that collar is regarded as his personal property for the term of his office, and cannot be worn by anyone deputising in his absence. In other provinces the collar is regarded as the insignia of a particular office and is worn by the brother undertaking those duties, whether he is the one who has been invested with it or a brother deputising for him in his absence. At Installation Meetings the normal practice is for those Past Masters temporarily occupying the officers of S W, J W and I G **not** to wear the collars of those offices. To do so would lead to practical difficulties later when the regular officers are being invested and the collars not be readily available.

New Masters are often unsure about when to wear the Master's collar. The Worshipful Master must always wear his collar at meetings of his own lodge, of Provincial Grand Lodge and Grand Lodge. The W M's collar is not worn when visiting other private lodges.

There are rarely problems about the regalia to be worn by members of the lodge, apart from collars as mentioned above. Visitors from other constitutions should wear the regalia of their constitution. Where a brother joins another constitution, such as a member of the Scottish Constitution joining an English Constitution lodge then the brother would wear the regalia of his English Lodge, whilst attending that Lodge.

Late arrivals
Having opened the Lodge and all the brethren being in their proper places, appropriately dressed, the first interruption to the planned routine is that of brethren arriving late and requesting admission. It is only necessary for the Master to welcome the brethren and this is conveniently done by a phrase such as "We greet you well".

The Gavel
The Master's gavel is an emblem of power to enable him to retain control in the Lodge. With the exception of parts of the installation ceremony, in most rituals the Master alone should use the gavel. Where the Lodge is being honoured by the visit of a representative of Grand Lodge or Provincial Grand Lodge, it is the usual custom to offer the gavel to the distinguished visitor. In this respect the Master should be familiar with Rules 122 to 124 B o C.

The only other occasion on which the Master hands over his gavel is when he vacates the Chair of King Solomon in favour of a Past Master to perform a ceremony. In such a case, the Master should sit on the immediate left of the Past-Master presiding. The I P M will then be seated on the immediate left of The Master, and the Chaplain on the I P M's immediate left, once more. The experienced Director of Ceremonies would have retained a spare chair to enable the line left of the Master to move along one place for this manoeuvre to be executed smoothly.

As has been mentioned earlier in connection with the Festive Board, excessive use of the gavel, and loud gavelling are to be avoided. Apart from the specific points in the ritual where the W M is required to gavel, the Master need only gavel to claim the attention of the brethren. If the Master has the attention of the brethren, then there is no need to gavel. Gentle gavelling does however, assist in identifying for the brethren the stage the Lodge business has reached. Loud gavelling can be most distressing to the senior brethren seated near to the Master's chair.

Proposals and Ballots
Formal proposals in Lodge require to be seconded and then put to the vote by a show of hands. The form of words most often used for such proposals

is "Brethren, you have all heard the proposal. Those in favour and who deem it worthy of confirmation please signify in the usual manner adopted among masons". The Master will then invite "Those to the contrary". In the unusual event that the votes for a particular proposal are equal, the Master shall give a second or casting vote — Rule 156 B o C.

In open Lodge and indeed in lodge committees, the business of the lodge is carried forward on the basis that it is the views of the majority of the brethren which prevail. This forms the basis of the strength of freemasonry. Although the views of senior members of the Lodge or of Founder members carry considerable weight in influencing the outcome, it is the views of the majority which matter in the end. Indeed, although the Master rules the Lodge he cannot decide what procedure shall be practised during his year of office. Rule 155 B o C lays down that the majority of the members regulate their own proceedings, **always providing that they are consistent with the laws and regulations of the Craft.**

Ballots frequently present difficulties for a new Master. Ballots are required for the election of certain officers and for membership of the Lodge. Ballots are normally taken by the completion by the brethren of ballot slips or by the use of 'Black balls'. The only exception to this rule is the election of the Tyler where the election is by show of hands.

The election of the Master and the Treasurer is usually by means of the ballot slip. Although there is normally only one stated candidate for these offices, every member is free to vote for any other qualified member if he so wishes. In checking the ballot slips the Master must ensure that all blank slips are rejected and must not be treated as votes for any particular candidate.

The ballot for membership of the Lodge is by custom the use of 'Black balls'. Whatever the arrangements for taking the ballot, the outcome is measured by the absence of 'Black balls'. Where black and white balls are used the outcome is literally determined by the absence or the number of black balls. Where two drawers are used and one colour of ball, it is the absence of balls from the 'Nay' drawer that determines the outcome. The new Master should refer to the Lodge bye-laws and ensure that he is familiar with the ruling before any meeting where a ballot is to be held, so as to avoid any misunderstanding.

The Book of Constitutions (Rule 165) states that "No person shall be made a mason in, or admitted a member of a Lodge, if on the ballot, three black balls appear against him; but the bye-laws of a Lodge may enact that two black balls or one black ball shall exclude a candidate; and the bye-laws may also enact that a reasonable period therein prescribed shall elapse before any rejected candidate can be proposed again in that Lodge''.

Most private lodges specify in their bye-laws the number of 'Black balls' and the number can vary quite markedly within the limits defined in the B o C. Where a ballot proves not to be in favour of the candidate then the ballot cannot be repeated on that night.

The interval which must elapse before a ballot can be taken again will be specified in the bye-laws usually of the order of six months. During the actual ballot for membership, the candidate being ballotted will not normally have entered the Lodge, or else will have been asked to retire during the short period that the ballot is in progress.

Harmony of the Lodge

Where a Master has good reason to believe that the continued presence of, or the admission of, a visiting brother into the Lodge would be disruptive, he may refuse that brother admission or ask him to leave — Rule 126.

Risings

The risings are a formal part of the closing of the Lodge. The risings ensure that any brother present has the opportunity to raise matters of interest to the Craft in general or that Lodge in particular, and to make proposals. The risings usually take the form as follows:

1. Communications from United Grand Lodge
2. Communications from Provincial Grand Lodge
3. Apologies for absence, correspondence and matters raised by the brethren.

In London Lodges the content of each rising is somewhat different and usually takes the form:

1. Communications from United Grand Lodge
2. Notices of motion and propositions for new and joining members
3. Apologies for absence, general matters raised by the brethren

At emergency meetings there are no risings since only the business on the summons can be transacted. Matters that might otherwise have arisen under the risings, therefore cannot be considered.

On completion of the risings, the Worshipful Master will then proceed to close the Lodge. The Lodge having been closed, it is the usual custom to sing the National Anthem and follow this with the closing hymn. The reason for this order of events has already been mentioned in Chapter 5.

Having closed the Lodge and left the Temple, the Master should not forget to give the warrant of the Lodge to the Secrtary for safe-keeping. A Master, can of course, retain the warrant in his own safe-keeping should he wish.

I have tried to identify the most frequent points which may arise in Lodge and can take a new Master unawares. A new Master is however, well advised to peruse the Book of Constitutions and that very helpful booklet "Information for the Guidance of Members of the Craft", at regular intervals. Such regular perusal will assist a Master should a difficulty arise.

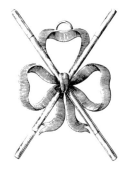

DIRECTOR OF CEREMONIES

Chapter Seven

LODGE COMMITTEES

IF THE BYE-LAWS PERMIT IT, and most do, the lodge may appoint a committee of its members. The function of the Lodge committee is to advise the Lodge on matters referred to that committee. One important function of such a committee is consideration of candidates, including the interviewing of such candidates, for membership of the Lodge.

The Worshipful Master normally chairs the committee meetings.

In the absence of the Master, the Chair should be taken by the Senior Warden, or if he is absent, by the Junior Warden or if he too is absent, the I P M.

It is a wise Master who gives some thought to the general principles of Chairmanship in order that he can run the meeting, so that all who wish to, are able to contribute to the discussion, and sound decisions when required are forthcoming.

The membership of the Lodge Committees is usually the Master, the Wardens, Past-Masters of and in the Lodge and the Treasurer and Secretary if they themselves are not past-masters. Many Lodges elect two lay brethren to the committee. The election of the lay brethren for this purpose is in open Lodge. Such lay brethren may not have voting rights.

The involvement of lay brethren in the work of the Lodge committee ensures that the role of the committee in the well-running of the Lodge is better understood by the majority of the brethren. There will be occasions when some matters discussed in committee require to be kept confidential. On the whole, however, it is best if the committee is not seen as a secret conclave, whose deliberations are too sensitive for those members of the lodge not eligible to attend.

The members of the committee can make proposals in the same way as in open Lodge. Such proposals require a seconder and are then voted on as in open Lodge. If the committee has lay members they may or may not have voting rights. In many lodges it is normally the latter.

To get the greatest benefit from Lodge Committee meetings, the Master should assist the Secretary to ensure that matters of importance are on the agenda for that meeting, and are not simply raised under 'Any other Business'. A carefully compiled agenda will ensure that the Secretary can check all relevant background information and come prepared to ensure that the discussion does not go astray or that unsound decisions are taken, due to inaccurate or insufficient information. Such preparation will assist the Master to chair the meeting effectively, so that the Lodge business is taken forward in an efficient manner.

SECRETARY

Chapter Eight

LODGE OF INSTRUCTION

THE IMPORTANCE OF mastering one or preferably two degree ceremonies before appointment as Warden has already been mentioned. There can be no doubt that there is no better way of preparing for mastership than that of attending lodge or class of instruction. During one's year as Master the L O I provides a forum in which the Master can perfect his skills with the objective of achieving a word-perfect performance in Temple.

If for any reason, such as one's employment, one cannot attend the L O I, of one's own Lodge regularly, it is perfectly in order to attend another L O I if that is more convenient. It is most important that the other L O I practises a similar working to that of one's own Lodge, otherwise confusion may result.

Attending another L O I does not of course, give the same advantages and benefits as that of one's own L O I; the teamwork so essential for success of any lodge cannot be fostered, nor does one have the opportunity to get to know all the members of the Lodge.

The key to success is unquestionably regular attendance at some L O I preferably your own. By such attendance the constant repetition will make the learning of the degree ceremonies much easier (but still not easy).

If a brother combines attendances at L O I with regular masonic reading he will be best able to discharge the duties of office and in so doing bring pleasure and satisfaction to himself and his brethren.

Those brethren interested in the difference between Lodge and Class of Instruction, please refer to the annex.

As with all masonic activities attendance at L O I is voluntary. The brethren will have done their best to 'get it right'. The Master will find that the brethren are only too happy to make such efforts if they can see that their hard work is appreciated. The Master should, therefore, make a point of thanking the brethren for their help and support at every appropriate opportunity.

PAST MASTER

Chapter Nine

UNITED GRAND LODGE OF ENGLAND

THE MEETINGS of the Quarterly Communications of United Grand Lodge of England are held at Great Queen Street in London, in March, June, September and December. All Masters, Wardens, and subscribing Past-Masters are eligible to attend. Rule 9 BoC.

It is strongly recommended that all Wardens and Masters attend United Grand Lodge during their term in office. Not only will they thereby represent their Lodge at the meeting, they will benefit from a better understanding of the working of Grand Lodge. Like most things masonic, understanding increases with actual partcipation in the activity.

On occasion one can, by attending the meeting, be part of masonic history in the making. An example of such a meeting was that of 11th June 1986 when the brethren in attendance voted to delete the traditional penalties from the Obligations in the ritual.

Grand Lodge has recently introduced a Newsletter which is circulated all members of the Craft in England. The *Newsletter* reports briefly on the main points raised at the last meeting of the Grand Lodge. Having attended the meeting, the Master and Wardens can at committee meetings, or indeed in open Lodge, add to the contents of the newsletter in terms of the discussion which may have taken place in Grand Lodge.

Brethren should at some stage in their masonic career visit the Grand Lodge buildings in Great Queen Street, and take part in the organised tours of the various temples and museum of Grand Lodge, which take place every day except Sunday. Non-masons may take part. Many wives and children of masons have found such tours a fascinating and enjoyable experience. (Further details of Grand Lodge in annex).

In the Provinces, meetings of Provincial Grand Lodges are held annually. All Masters, Wardens, Past-Masters and Master masons are eligible to attend and are strongly encouraged to do so. Again, attendance at meetings of their Provincial Grand Lodge allows brethren to participate in the activities of the Province.

Chapter Ten

LADIES' NIGHTS

THE LADIES' NIGHT, or dinner and dance held annually by many, if not most lodges, is outside Lodge business. A Ladies' night is not, strictly, speaking, a masonic function and must be handled quite separately from the masonic business of the Lodge. Having said that, it is not surprising that the lay public see such functions as masonic since they are normally organised by masons with the Worshipful Master as the President for the evening.

The long established custom of holding an annual dinner and dance is to be commended for a number of reasons. It is for example, one way of a brother showing his appreciation to his lady for her understanding and support for his masonic activities during the previous year. It is also a way of involving the ladies in a social evening so that masonic friendships may be widened. Many valuable masonic friendships valuable to the individual mason and to masonry in general, have resulted from introductions during a Ladies' Night. It forms a useful way of screening potential candidates into masonry, since it offers a means of getting to know the individual in a relaxed environment. There have been many excellent brethren who first developed an interest in Freemasonry from having been invited to a Ladies' Night by a mason, but often at that stage with no ulterior motive.

The Ladies' Night is usually organised by one or two brethren who form the Festival Committee. The Master by accepting the Presidency for that evening, assumes considerable responsibility for the function, including the financial responsibility. Despite the importance of such events for the life of a lodge, the lodge has no responsibility for the function.

In view of the importance of such functions for a lodge, and that importance should not be underestimated, a Master anxious to do his best for his lodge should perhaps consider the Ladies' Night as a legitimate part of his year, albeit a 'non-masonic' part of his year.

Chapter Eleven

PREPARATION FOR THE INSTALLATION OF THE MASTER-ELECT

W HEN THE TIME APPROACHES to install one's successor into the Chair of King Solomon, attention is obviously concentrated on the ceremony itself. Since this will also be the last ceremony he will perform during his mastership of the lodge, it is also the one for which he is likely to be remembered. A Master is well advised to ensure that all goes well on his last meeting.

The Master will have available to him all the assistance he could desire from the Director of Ceremonies and the Secretary in his preparation for the meeting. Apart from the ritual of the actual ceremony there are a few practical points which the Master will wish to consider and cover.

The Master will wish to reflect, with the Secretary and D C on the past-masters who will assist in the ceremony by occupying the chairs of S W, J W, and another to act as Inner Guard during the ceremony of Installation.

Early in the ceremony the Master invites all his officers to line up in the North, prior to passing round the Lodge, thereby giving him the opportunity to thank each for his support during the year. It is important to remember to ask the officers to line up in order of seniority. This is not done out of a sense of hierarchy or regimentation, but from the practical viewpoint, that by doing so, the collars of office are collected in the correct sequence for the subsequent part of the ceremony. There is nothing more annoying than to have the appointment and investiture of officers delayed whilst the D C or A D C searches for the appropriate collar.

The importance of being as expert as possible, and as near word-perfect as one can achieve in the degree ceremonies, is principally for the candidate's benefit. A candidate only goes through a degree ceremony once and the better the ceremony is performed, the more profound will be the effect on the candidate and the longer will that effect persist. At the Installation meeting, the candidate on this occasion is an experienced mason, albeit still in ignorance with respect to the inner workings, and his perception of the skill with which the ceremony is performed is that much greater. The Installing Master therefore, owes it to his successor to be as expert as humanly possible on this very special occasion.

Back to practical points in the ceremony — it is a wise step for the Installing Master to take off the gauntlets just prior to opening the Board of Installed Masters. At the stage when one has just placed the new Master in the Chair of King Solomon, remember to pause so as to give the Master the opportunity to put his gloves back on and put on the gauntlets. It may seem a small point but it can be disconcerting to the Master who will feel the need to wear gloves, but will not know how to do so if not offered such a prompt. Any such distraction can mar that part of the ceremony for the Master.

At the close of the Board of Installed Masters those present will wish to congratulate the new Master, and as will be discovered by visiting other Lodges, there are various ways of doing this. To ensure that this part of the installation goes smoothly, it is essential to agree, before the meeting begins, the manner in which it will be done.

In some workings the Installing Master delivers the Address to the Master at the completion of the ceremony. What better way to end the ceremony than to have the privilege of delivering this address.

The Installing Master having discharged his duties and the installation being completed, he now takes up his duties of the Immediate Past Master. It is to the I P M that the W M will turn should he require a prompt. The I P M must be ready to guide the Master gently through this, his first meeting, and later at the Festive Board.

In some lodges it is the custom to present a breast jewel to the outgoing master as a token of appreciation for the way in which he managed the lodge affairs during his year. It is most important to remember that this is not his right, but rather it is a gift from the brethren. The I P M should therefore be ready to say a few appropriate words of thanks to the brethren. Simply to accept the breast jewel and sit down can have an adverse effect, and spoil the Installing Master's efforts up to this point.

Chapter Twelve

ROYAL ARCH FREEMASONRY

IT IS THE INTENTION here only to draw attention to the crucial role the Order of the Holy Royal Arch plays with respect to Craft masonry. Royal Arch is not a separate fourth degree. The authority for so stating is Grand Lodge, for the Board of General Purposes of Grand Lodge recommend that all brethren should be reminded that the completion of the third degree of a master mason includes the supreme order of the Holy Royal Arch and that the brethren should be encouraged to complete their Craft masonry by seeking Exaltation in a Royal Arch Chapter. Many brethren find the statement that the Royal Arch is the completion of the Third Degree rather difficult to understand particuarly those brethren who have not yet been Exalted.

A brother cannot be exalted until he has been a master mason for four weeks or more. If he wishes to progress, then it is suggested that his Exaltation should have taken place by the time the brother has completed three years as a master mason.

In practice all this means is that every Master will normally be a member of the Royal Arch. As stated earlier, a Master who has not been exalted is at a disadvantage since his masonic knowledge and experience is incomplete. Apart from the desirability of Exaltation in order to complete a brother's understanding of the three Craft degrees, there can be little doubt that the experience will be enjoyable and will give the brother a sense of masonic achievement and completeness.

PAST MASTER

Chapter Thirteen

USEFUL INFORMATION

United Grand Lodge and Freemasons Hall

It is worth repeating that the Quarterly Communications of the United Grand Lodge of England are held at noon precisely on the second Wednesday in March, June, September and December. The brethren who are eligible to attend include all Grand Officers (Present and Past), Masters, Wardens and Past-Masters of lodges held under the English Constitution — Rule 9 BoC. This reminder is given to brethren eligible to attend so that they may be able to plan a visit to the building, library and museum, in conjunction with a visit to Grand Lodge.

Freemasons Hall in Great Queen Street, London is a fine example of British architecture. There are many features of the building, such as the Bronze doors to the Grand Temple which weigh 2½ tons, which in themselves make a visit to Great Queen Street well worth while. There are a total of nineteen temples. The Grand Temple and other temples together can seat 4,000 brethren. There is also a fine library and museum. There is also now a permanent exhibition on the History of English Freemasonry. Freemasons Hall is open to the public daily from 10am to 5pm, Saturday 10am to 1pm, Sundays, Public Holidays excepted. There are normally conducted tours of the building, including the Grand Temple, hourly from 11am to 4pm Monday to Friday, and by special arrangement on Saturdays.

Lodges of Instruction

An essential feature of any successful lodge is the provision of a meeting place where the brethren can meet regularly and practise the ritual. Such a meeting place normally takes the form of a lodge or class of instruction. It is probably true to say that the majority of lodges favour the latter for practical reasons.

A lodge of instruction can only be held under the sanction of a Lodge, by licence and authority of the Grand Master. The Lodge or licence holder is responsible for ensuring that the proceedings are in accord with the tenets of the Craft. The conditions which must be met regarding the setting up of a Lodge of instruction, the need to obtain approval of the time and place of meetings, and the keeping of minutes etc are dealt with in the BoC under

Rules 132-135.

In comparision with a lodge of instruction, a Class of Instruction is much less formal, and indeed has no formal status in relation to any Lodge. In many, if not most, cases the informality relates only to the failure to comply with the BoC, in every other respect, the class of instruction is run on very formal terms mimicking a regular lodge meeting. It has to be admitted that a class of instruction, since it is not required to meet any formal standards as set out in the BoC, can become something of a club. It is perhaps true to say that any form of regular meeting, however informal, where the ritual is practised is better than none, provided of course, that every effort is made to avoid erroneous and bad practice of the ritual.

The premier lodge of instruction under the English constitution must be the Emulation Lodge of Improvement. The Emulation Lodge of Improvement was established as a master masons' lodge in October 1823. The function of the lodge was to demonstrate to master masons the Emulation working of the degree ceremonies and to lecture the brethren on masonic matters, The lodge has met regularly since its establishment, meetings are held at Freemasons Hall, Great Queen Street, London every Friday evening, October to June. The fact that the Lodge meets in London, means of course, that many interested master masons throughout England are unable to attend. With the objective of maintaining high standards of Emulation working of masonic ritual, arrangements exist for private lodges of instruction to be recognised by the committee of the Emulation Lodge of Improvement. To be so recognised, certain criteria must be met, which include the following: the Preceptor must be approved by the committee of the Emulation Lodge of Improvement; the lodge of instruction must have bye-laws embodying strict conditions for the running of the lodge of instruction which must be acceptable to the committee of the Emulation Lodge of Improvement; and a subscription together with a report must be made annually to the committee of the Emulation Lodge of Improvement.

Quatuor Coronati Correspondence Circle

If one were looking for a college or institution of academic freemasonry one might consider the Quatuor Coronati Lodge and the associated correspondence circle as fulfilling that function.

The Quatuor Coronati Lodge No 2076 was established by warrant in November 1884 and was consecrated in 1886. The lodge was designed to promote the study of Masonic Archaeology and named after the four crowned martyrs mentioned in early masonic manuscripts. In ancient times the craft of a stonemason was known as Ars Quatuor Coronatorum, hence the martyrs were known as Quatuor Coronati.

In the early years of the lodge a literary society was formed which was known as the Outer Circle or Correspondence Circle. The interest in the Correspondence Circle has continued to the point where there are now some 14,000 members. From the many papers and lectures given each year, Transactions are compiled. These Transactions are now published annually but in the past some volumes have covered a number of years. To any mason interested in the history and evolution of Freemasonry, these volumes form a valuable source of reference. Anyone interested in studying the history of the Quatuor Coronati Lodge is recommended to refer to the booklet prepared by Colin Dyer to mark the centenary of the Lodge (the History of the first 100 years of the Quatuor Coronati Lodge No 2076 — Colin Dyer).

Membership of the Correspondence Circle is recommended to any serious student of Freemasonry. Members receive all lodge summonses which include questions and answers on masonic subjects, a copy of the annual volume of the Transactions, and among other features can submit questions on masonic history, custom or ritual which will be answered by experts.

Further details can be obtained from:
Q,C,C,C, Ltd,
60 Great Queen Street, London WC2B 5AZ

The Dormer Masonic Study Circle

Of more recent origin and perhaps less well known is the Dormer Study Circle established in 1938. The aim of the circle is to teach and uphold the highest ideals of Freemasonry, and to increase the knowledge, understanding and appreciation of masonry by their members. Meetings are held at Freemasons Hall, Great Queen Street, each month, usually on a Saturday between 2 and 5pm. The Circle has a masonic library from which members can obtain books on loan. Quarterly Communications are circulated to members together with the Transactons, which are normally four per year. The Transactions contain a selection of the papers read at the Circle meetings.

Further details can be obtained from:
Peter B Land,
23A Compton Avenue,
East Ham, London E6 3DR

The London Grand Rank Association

The London Grand Rank Association was established for holders of London Grand Rank. Meetings of the Association are held each quarter at Conway Hall, Red Lion Square, London. The Association offers many services to its members. In 1975 the Association introduced Bulletin Subscription so that masons who did not hold L G R could join and receive the very informative Quarterly Bulletin. This bulletin like the other communications mentioned above contains much information on points of masonic interest and for the small subscription fee it is very good value.

Further details from:

The Secretary,
London Grand Rank Association,
P O Box 324
60 Great Queen Street,
London WC2B 5AZ

The Royal Masonic Hospital

There can be few brethren who do not know of the excellent work that the Royal Masonic Hospital provides for masons and their dependants in terms of health care. Few masons will be unaware of the hospital's financial plight. What is not so well known is the fact that the Hospital will organise Official Visits for Lodges or Guided Tours of the hospital for interested parties. A guided tour arranged for the brethren of the Lodge and their dependants would make an interesting day out and would increase the appreciation by the brethren of the work done by, and potential of, the hospital.

Further details:

The Secretary,
The Royal Masonic Hospital,
Ravenscourt Park,
London W6 0TN

TYLER